Diane OJ.   X

BRUCE &

POCKET GUIDE TO

SHARING
YOUR
FAITH

BRUCE BICKEL and STAN JANTZ

HARVEST HOUSE PUBLISHERS
Eugene, Oregon 97402

Cover design by Left Coast Design, Portland, Oregon

Other books by the guys:

Bruce & Stan's® Guide to God
Bruce & Stan's® Guide to the Bible
Bruce & Stan's® Guide to Bible Prophecy
Bruce & Stan's® Pocket Guide to Talking with God
God Is in the Small Stuff (and It All Matters)
God Is in the Small Stuff for Your Family
God Is in the Small Stuff for Your Marriage
Onyourown.com—e-mail messages to my daughter
Real Life Begins After High School

BRUCE & STAN'S® POCKET GUIDE TO SHARING YOUR FAITH
Copyright © 2000 by Bruce Bickel and Stan Jantz
Published by Harvest House Publishers
Eugene, Oregon 97402

Library of Congress Cataloging-in-Publication Data
Bickel, Bruce, 1952–
    [Pocket guide to sharing your faith]
    Bruce & Stan's pocket guide to sharing your faith / Bruce Bickel
    and Stan Jantz.
        p. cm.
    ISBN 0-7369-0270-8
    1. Witness bearing (Christianity)   I. Title: Bruce and Stan's pocket guide to
sharing your faith.   II. Jantz, Stan, 1952–   III. Title.
BV4520 B513 20000
248'.5—dc21   00-022230

Printed in the United States of America.

01 02 03 04 05 06 07 08 09 / BP / 10 9 8 7 6 5 4 3 2

Contents

A Note from the Authors

It is a very common situation. You and a friend are sitting in the local Starbucks at a stylish table that is about the size of a hubcap. While your friend takes a sip of Brazilian Rain Forest coffee, you let your latte cool and start chatting about the activities and issues of life. The conversation flows so naturally. Your discussion covers everything from personal relationships to world events. There is an interesting mix of political commentary, human-interest stories, and sports and entertainment analysis. Sort of CNN mixed with *Regis & Kathie Lee* (although neither of you is as boisterous as Kathie Lee, or the Starbucks manager would ask you to sit outside).

All of a sudden, the tranquility of the moment is abruptly interrupted. Your friend breaks the unwritten rule of conversational etiquette by shifting the topic into the realm of . . . RELIGION. There were no evil intentions on your friend's part to make you feel awkward—it was just an innocent question about why *you* prefer to go to church on Sunday mornings rather than sleep late and read the Sunday newspaper in your pajamas until noon. Hey, it's an honest question. Inquiring minds want to know. But your body goes into a spastic seizure at the thought of having to talk about your faith in God. Your blood pressure rises so fast that you can actually hear the corpuscles swooshing through your veins. Beads of sweat are forming on your forehead. Your tongue starts to swell, pushing saliva bubbles out of your mouth. (You hope that your friend will think this is just a "foam mustache" from the latte.)

As your brain goes into hyper-drive to review theological concepts of the Trinity and appropriate verses to present a four-step plan of salvation, your friend says, "I'm only asking because I need to know if you get a Sunday newspaper. Last week there was a '2-for-1' coupon at Fat-Burger, and I'd like yours if you aren't going to use it." You breathe a sigh of relief. Although you had clipped the coupon, you are more than glad to forfeit a free burger to avoid discussing your relationship with God.

Do You Love Walking with God but Fear Talking About God?

Although we haven't personally met you, we have a pretty good idea of who you are and what you're like:

• First of all, we think it's safe to assume that you're a Christian.

• Second, we're sure that you enjoy being around other Christians and talking about God.

• Third, while it is easy for you to talk about God with other Christians, you freeze up when it comes to talking about Him to non-Christians.

• Finally, we suspect that you feel guilty about this. Your friends need to know about God, but you never really talk to them about Him.

You've got to be asking yourself how two regular guys like us can have such keen insights into your life. For starters, the very fact that you're reading this book tells us that you want to know more about sharing your faith. We also suspect that you're no different from most other Christians. You love God, but you're reluctant to talk about Him. You may even be afraid.

This Book Is for You If . . .

We wrote this book to help you discover that talking about God doesn't have to be something you fear. It can be as natural as breathing. The problem is that you have some misconceptions about what it takes to share your faith. See if you can identify with this list—

✔ You are a new Christian and you are excited about Jesus, but you think that you shouldn't say anything until you know a lot more about all of this God stuff.

✔ You have been a Christian for a long time—so long that you have forgotten how to talk about Jesus without using theological terms. It is a mystery to you why your neighbors aren't interested in God when you explain salvation with phrases like: "The redemption that comes from justification begins our sanctification that is complete at our glorification."

✔ You are afraid that someone might ask questions that you can't answer. You aren't worried that your faith will be shaken, but you just don't want to embarrass God with a bunch of "Duh, I don't know" responses.

✔ You don't mind making a public statement about God, but it will have to be without words. You just aren't a public speaker. You have resigned yourself to keeping your mouth shut. Instead, you'll do your witnessing with a WWJD bracelet and a bumper sticker that reads: "Caution—this car will be driverless in the event of the rapture."

✔ You've got all of the "How to be a Christian" verses marked in your Bible, and you even have a little "plan of salvation" outline written on the inside cover. But you'd be afraid to talk to someone about God unless you had your Bible with you. This rules out sharing your faith with someone at the checkout line in the grocery store.

✔ You think that you've got to memorize a whole bunch of Bible verses before you talk to anyone about God. You are really worried about this, because you can't even memorize your personal identification number for your bank's ATM machine.

✔ You think that you don't have an interesting "testimony." You grew up in a Christian home, and your life has been pretty uneventful. You think sharing your faith would be easier if you had a more dramatic conversion experience.

This Book Is Interactive

Well, the *book* isn't interactive, but we are. We didn't want to just write this book and then walk away. We would like to stay involved in the process as you read through the book. (You know, like someone who is always looking over your shoulder and annoying you with questions as you try to read. Hey, if you can do the reading, we can do the annoying.) Here's how we propose to keep this book interactive:

- **Icons.** From time to time, we'll leave an icon in the margin to help you identify what you're reading:

Big Idea—This is a main point. You can skip other stuff, but this is important.

Key Verse—Notice we didn't say "important." All Bible verses are important, but we'll let you know the ones that have particular relevance to the topic of sharing your faith.

Glad You Asked—See, we aren't afraid of your questions. We even try to anticipate them.

It's a Mystery—You will be relieved to know that you aren't responsible for explaining everything about God. There are some things about God that remain a mystery and can't be explained or understood.

Learn the Lingo—There are some pretty deep theological concepts involved with your faith. We'll try to explain in layman's language some of the more technical terminology.

Dig Deeper—We have learned a lot about sharing our faith from other authors. At the end of each chapter, we'll give you the names of some of our favorite books that might be of further help to you.

- **Tell Us What You Are Thinking.** We would love to hear your comments about this book. (We prefer compliments to criticism, but we accept both.) Actually, we are most interested in hearing about how you are learning to share your faith. What works for you? What happed in the life of the person who you talked to? Let us know. We promise that you'll hear back from us. You can reach us at:
  Email: *guide@bruceandstan.com*
  Website: *www.bruceandstan.com*
  Snail Mail: Bruce & Stan
                     P.O. Box 25565,
                     Fresno CA 93729-5565

Think About It This Way

People talk with each other about everything: politics, movies, restaurants, shopping, sports, our families, and our jobs. Sometimes we talk about important things, and sometimes we dwell on the trivial.

Often we don't even know much about what we are talking about (which is our situation if the subject was "automobile repair"). But whatever it is, talking about these things comes naturally, as naturally as . . . well, *talking*.

Your personal relationship with God is the most important part of your life. It is only natural that you should be talking with other people about it. And that's exactly how you should be when you do it—natural.

So relax and start reading. Before you know it, you'll be back sitting at Starbucks. And when your friend brings up the subject of God, you will be able to respond naturally about your personal relationship with Jesus (without choking so hard that your latte comes out your nose).

Chapter 1

DO YOU HAVE A CHOICE?
WHY SHARING YOUR FAITH IS NOT AN OPTION

> *There is no nobler calling, no better investment of one's life, than telling others how to know God personally and enjoy Him forever.*
>
> —Bill Bright

Living the Christian life is both the easiest and the hardest thing you'll ever do. It's easy because there's nothing you can do to earn God's special favor. There's no application process to becoming a Christian, and there's nothing you can do to qualify. God loves you because He is God, and He saves you because of Jesus Christ. Once you give your life to Jesus, your eternal future is secure.

The Christian life is also hard because God doesn't want you to just sit there and wait for heaven. He's asked you to do certain things, the most important of which is to tell others about what He has done for you. That's what sharing your faith is all about, and that's what this book is all about. Sharing your faith should be the most natural thing in the world. But it's often very difficult, mainly because we don't really understand it.

By the end of this first chapter, we hope you do understand what it means to share your faith, and we pray that you will be ready to take the next step.

Bruce & Stan

Chapter 1

Do You Have a Choice?
Why Sharing Your Faith
Is Not an Option

. . . .

What's Ahead

➤ The Greatest Gift in the World
➤ What Does It Mean to Share Your Faith?
➤ Why Does God Leave It Up to Us?
➤ There's a Method to God's Plan
➤ The Great Commission
➤ Having the Heart of Jesus
➤ Salvation Is for Everyone

. . . .

What's the greatest gift you ever received? It certainly wasn't that belt sander your husband gave you for your anniversary, or the extra large bottle of mouthwash your friends wrapped up for your last birthday. Your most memorable gift was probably something like that red bike you got for Christmas as a kid, or the car your dad gave you for graduation. Or maybe it was a bouquet of flowers sent by someone very special.

15

When you receive an unexpected and truly wonderful gift, you experience a whole range of emotions. You are surprised, delighted, and grateful as you look at and think about this thoughtful thing someone has done for you. And then, once you settle down and realize exactly what you have, you are compelled to tell someone—anyone. You tell your family, you call your friends, and you even show off your gift to perfect strangers. It's all part of the experience of receiving a great gift.

The Greatest Gift in the World

You could stack up all the terrific gifts you have received in your lifetime. In fact, you could collect all the great gifts ever given to people everywhere for all time, and they wouldn't begin to compare to the single greatest gift in the world, given to you by the God of the universe—the gift of salvation.

God saved you by his special favor when you believed. And you can't take credit for this; it is a gift from God (Ephesians 2:8).

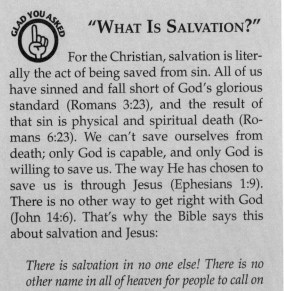

"WHAT IS SALVATION?"

For the Christian, salvation is literally the act of being saved from sin. All of us have sinned and fall short of God's glorious standard (Romans 3:23), and the result of that sin is physical and spiritual death (Romans 6:23). We can't save ourselves from death; only God is capable, and only God is willing to save us. The way He has chosen to save us is through Jesus (Ephesians 1:9). There is no other way to get right with God (John 14:6). That's why the Bible says this about salvation and Jesus:

There is salvation in no one else! There is no other name in all of heaven for people to call on to save them (Acts 4:12).

Salvation Is a Gift, Not a Secret

The qualities of your salvation are very much like the qualities of a gift—

- A gift always has benefits.

- A gift suggests a personal connection between the giver and the receiver.

- When you receive a gift, you naturally want to share it with others.

On the other hand, salvation and secrecy have nothing in common—

- Few secrets have benefits.

- There's rarely a connection between the person who told you the secret and the secret itself.

- When someone tells you a secret, you're supposed to keep it to yourself.

Yet many people treat salvation like it's some kind of secret. They know what a wonderful thing they have, but they're reluctant to tell others. They may even be afraid. Why do you think this happens? We think it has to do with a misunderstanding of what it means to share your faith.

What Does It Mean to Share Your Faith?

The phrase that we're using in this book to describe the process of talking about God and what it means to receive the gift of salvation is *sharing your faith*. The Bible never actually uses that phrase. Instead, the Bible uses words like—

- **Witness**
  "You will receive power when the Holy Spirit comes on you; and you will be my witnesses in Jerusalem, and in all Judea and Samaria, and to the ends of the earth" (Acts 1:8 NIV).

- **Evangelize**
  He is the one who gave these gifts to the church: the apostles, the prophets, the evangelists, and the pastors and teachers (Ephesians 4:11).

- **Preach the Good News**
  And then he told them, "Go into all the world and preach the Good News to everyone, everywhere" (Mark 16:15).

- **Tell Them**
  "Go home to your friends, and tell them what wonderful things the Lord has done for you and how merciful he has been" (Mark 5:19).

> **"Good News"**
> In the Bible, "good news" and the "gospel" are the same thing. They both describe salvation in Jesus. That's why you'll sometimes hear people talk about "spreading the good news" or "preaching the gospel."

- **Let Your Light Shine**
  "Don't hide your light under a basket! Instead, put it on a stand and let it shine for all" (Matthew 5:15).

- **Show Others**
  This is so you can show others the goodness of God, for he called you out of the darkness into his wonderful light (1 Peter 2:9).

- **Plant Seeds**
  My job was to plant the seed in your hearts, and Apollos watered it, but it was God, not we, who made it grow (1 Corinthians 3:6).

SHARING YOUR FAITH IS LIKE PLANTING SEEDS

The Bible often compares sharing your faith to planting seeds. Jesus told the story of a farmer scattering some seed (Luke 8:5-15). "The seed is God's message," Jesus explained, and we are the farmer. Just like there's nothing a farmer can do to make the seed grow, there's nothing we can do to make the good news take root in a life. Only God can make His message grow.

If you were to look up all of these words and phrases in *Strong's Concordance* (a very useful book) you would find something very interesting. All of them involve *declaring, proclaiming, reporting, showing, scattering, speaking,* and *publishing* the Good News about Jesus Christ and what He has done for us. In other words, *sharing your faith!*

The problem is that many of us think sharing our faith involves *convincing, convicting,* and *converting.* No wonder we're afraid! Who wants to take on that kind of responsibility? Well, you can relax, because God doesn't expect us to do any of that. We couldn't convince, convict, and convert anyone, even if we tried. Only God can do these things:

- The love of God through Christ *convinces* us (Romans 8:38).

- The work of God through the Holy Spirit *convicts* us (John 16:8 NIV).

- The grace of God through our faith *converts* us (1 Corinthians 3:7).

Sharing your faith should be the most natural thing in the world, because it's really nothing more than telling someone else the story of what God has done for you. When you talk about Jesus with one other person, you are sharing your faith. When you tell the story of your spiritual journey in front of a group (even if your knees are knocking), you are sharing your faith. When you tell people about Jesus in a letter or e-mail—or you give them a book about Jesus—you are sharing your faith.

The reason many of us are reluctant to share our faith is that we worry about what other people will say or do. We're afraid they might say no. We think we might be ridiculed. We are concerned that we might offend someone. Don't worry about it! Sharing your faith isn't about you. Sharing your faith isn't even about the other person saying yes, no, or maybe. It's all about God and His incredible gift to us. All He wants us to do is share the gift. He promises to do the rest.

Why Does God Leave It Up to Us?

 In many ways, God is a mystery (He wouldn't be God if we could completely figure Him out). Take the gift of salvation, for example. If it were up to us humans, we'd probably lay the gift out there like flu shots in a clinic. Stand in line, pay your $5, and be done with it. But God has another idea. He wants us to tell others. He wants us to share our faith. Why would He do this? Why would God entrust this very important job—telling unsaved people about the greatest gift in the world—to us? That's a huge responsibility!

"WHY DOESN'T GOD DO IT HIMSELF?"

You might be wondering, hey, if salvation is so important (and it is), why doesn't God tell everyone Himself? Well, He has, in at least four different ways that we can think of:

1. God has placed the truth about Himself in the *heart* of every human being (Romans 1:19).

2. God has placed the truth about Himself in *nature* (Romans 1:20).

3. God has placed the truth about Himself in the *Bible* (2 Timothy 3:15,16).

4. God has placed the truth about Himself in *Jesus* (John 10:30; 14:9).

There's a Method to God's Plan

There are some very good reasons why God wants us to share our faith. These reasons have to do with our ultimate purpose, God's ultimate plan, and God's chosen path:

Our Ultimate Purpose

Do you ever wonder why you exist in the first place? You should! It's the number one question people have asked through the ages. (The second most popular question is: "Did Adam have a navel?") And here's the number one answer:

For everything comes from him; everything exists by his power and is intended for his glory. To him be glory evermore. Amen (Romans 11:36).

There you have it. You exist in order to glorify God. That's why God created you. And when you talk to others about God, you glorify Him, whether they respond or not.

God's Ultimate Plan

God isn't some old gray-haired man sitting on a cloud in heaven, waiting to zap us when we do wrong. Neither is He a big benign celestial Santa Claus who only looks at the good stuff we do. God is the holy, dynamic, personal, loving Creator of the universe. He made us to glorify Him and to enjoy Him. But He can't relate to us as long as our lives are characterized by sin. So God made a way for us to come back to Him through Jesus. This is His ultimate plan:

> *His unchanging plan has always been to adopt us into his own family by bringing us to himself through Jesus Christ. And this gave him great pleasure* (Ephesians 1:5).

This is what God wants you to share with others. The essence of your faith is Jesus, and when you share it, God is pleased.

God's Chosen Path

See how this works? God created us to glorify Him, but sin cut us off from God. So God revealed His plan, which was to bring us back to Him through the death and resurrection of His Son, Jesus. That's the gift of salvation.

When we receive the gift by faith, we automatically become a part of all believers everywhere, collectively known as the church. As a member of this universal church (also known as the body of Christ), we have an obligation to—

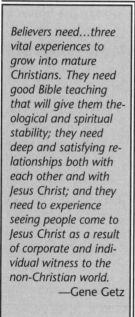

Believers need...three vital experiences to grow into mature Christians. They need good Bible teaching that will give them theological and spiritual stability; they need deep and satisfying relationships both with each other and with Jesus Christ; and they need to experience seeing people come to Jesus Christ as a result of corporate and individual witness to the non-Christian world.
—Gene Getz

• Worship God (Ephesians 5:16-19)

• Serve one another (Ephesians 4:12)

• Share our faith (Mark 16:15)

The Great Commission

We hope you are beginning to realize that sharing your faith is not an option for the believer. It's not just for pastors, missionaries, Sunday school teachers, or TV evangelists. *Sharing your faith is the responsibility and the privilege of every single person who has called on Jesus to save him or her.*

If you need more convincing, all you have to do is read the last words Jesus spoke while on earth. All four of Jesus' biographers wrote down these words, which have become known as the Great Commission:

- Matthew recorded the best-known statement of the Great Commission, where the emphasis is on the authority of Christ (Matthew 28:19).

- Mark was very clear that anyone who rejects the Good News will be condemned (Mark 16:15,16).

- Luke reminds us that Jesus fulfilled prophecy by coming to earth and dying for our sins (Luke 24:46,47).

- John wrote that Jesus was commissioned to be a light to the world, and so are we (John 20:21).

- Finally, in the book of Acts (also written by Luke) we learn that the Great Commission is no empty command. Jesus has given us the power to share our faith:

"When the Holy Spirit has come upon you, you will receive power and will tell people about me everywhere—in Jerusalem, throughout Judea, in Samaria, and to the ends of the earth" (Acts 1:8).

By the way, notice that Jesus' words are not called the Great *Suggestion* or the Great *Idea*. This is a *commission*, which is defined as "written order giving certain powers, privileges, and duties." That's exactly what Jesus has laid out for us. Make no mistake about it. *Sharing your faith is not an option.*

Having the Heart of Jesus

Our salvation is based on the person and work of Jesus, "on whom our faith depends from start to finish" (Hebrews 12:2).

Doesn't it make sense that we should not only follow Jesus, but also imitate Him in all we do?

There's no question about it. We need to live like Jesus would live. We need to have the heart of Jesus, which came out in the life He lived here on earth. When you study the life of Christ in the Bible, here's what you find:

- ✔ Jesus came to earth to save us, not condemn us (John 3:17). We are already dead in our sins, but God offers the free gift of eternal life through Jesus (Romans 6:23).

- ✔ Jesus doesn't want anyone to die in their sins. He wants as many people to be saved as possible. In fact, He is delaying His return so that more people will be saved (2 Peter 3:9).

- ✔ Jesus is praying for everyone who will eventually believe in Him (John 17:20).

> *Live your life the way Jesus would live your life if He had your life to live.*
> —Dallas Willard

The heart of Jesus breaks for the lost. He died for all people, but only those who believe in Him can have eternal life (John 3:16). Just like Jesus, our hearts need to break for people without Christ. We need to see people without Christ—whether they are our friends, neighbors, co-workers, family members, or complete strangers—as people without hope. They have a fatal disease called sin, and the only cure is Christ. We know that, and we need to tell them.

Salvation Is for Everyone

There's no person Christ can't save. God loves every person who has ever lived, and He has made His salvation available to anyone who asks:

Anyone who calls on the name of the Lord will be saved (Romans 10:13).

> *Winners of souls must first be weepers of souls.*
> —C. H. Spurgeon

But there's a catch, a condition. Others won't know unless we tell them! Unless we share our faith, they won't believe. It's as simple and as serious as that.

But how can they call on him to save them unless they believe in him? And how can they believe in him if they have never heard about him? And how can they hear about him unless someone tells them? And how will anyone go and tell them without being sent? That is what the Scriptures mean when they say, "How beautiful are the feet of those who bring good news!" (Romans 10:14,15).

What's That Again?

1. The greatest gift in the world is salvation through Jesus Christ.

2. Sharing your faith is telling the story of what God has done for you.

3. God wants you to share your faith because it involves His purpose, His plan, and His path for you.

4. The Great Commission is a written order given to you by Jesus to share your faith with others.

5. When you have the heart of Jesus, your heart will break for the lost.

Dig Deeper

Here are some of our favorite books about sharing your faith.

How to Share Your Faith by Greg Laurie, the pastor of a huge church that has grown primarily through people sharing their faith.

Witnessing Without Fear by Bill Bright. This book will show you how to share your faith with confidence.

The Master Plan of Discipleship by Robert E. Coleman shows how the disciples fulfilled the Great Commission, and how we can do the same today.

Moving On

Salvation may be a gift, but sharing that gift with others is not simply a matter of saying to someone, "Here, take it." You need to be ready to explain what it means to be saved, and that means you need to know something about your faith and how it works. In the next chapter we'll tell you how important it is to study God's Word while relying on the power of the Holy Spirit.

Chapter 2

SPIRITUAL BOOT CAMP:
GET YOUR MIND INTO SHAPE

> *If you cannot express yourself well on each of your beliefs, work and study until you can. If you don't, other people may miss out on the blessings that come from knowing the truth. Strive to re-express a truth of God to yourself clearly and understandably, and God will use that same explanation when you share it with someone else.*
>
> —Oswald Chambers

Just like it's no fun to play sports or exercise when you're out of physical shape, it's frustrating to live the Christian life when you're out of spiritual shape. In this chapter you will learn how to get your mind in tune with the mind of Christ, who wants you to give Him nothing less than your best.

By studying God's Word and allowing the Holy Spirit to control your life, you will add energy and excitement to your life as a believer. More importantly, you will have an impact on those around you as you share your faith with new power and understanding.

Bruce & Stan

Chapter 2

Spiritual Boot Camp: Get Your Mind into Shape

. . . .

What's Ahead

➤ Preparing Yourself
➤ Developing the Skills
➤ Basic Training Part I—The Word of God
➤ Basic Training Part II—The Spirit of God
➤ Know What You Believe
➤ How to Share the Gift of Salvation

. . . .

We used to think a Navy Seal was a trained sea creature that performed for the amphibious branch of the armed forces. Then we met David, a real Navy Seal.

What we discovered is that David is one of a very select group of highly skilled and supremely fit military people (not unlike Bruce & Stan) who train for years to defend our country. The way they prepare for their specialized roles—which includes, but is not limited to, blowing stuff up underwater and going for weeks without food or sleep—is astounding. By the time they graduate from Seal School, these guys are ready to answer the call at any time and in any situation.

Preparing Yourself

Meeting David got us to thinking about our role and our fitness as Christians. What kind of shape are we in? How skilled are we in the details of the Christian life? Are we prepared for any situation—including, but not limited to, sharing our faith at Starbucks? Well, we certainly don't measure up to the standards of David the Seal in his *physical* fitness and preparedness. But why can't we have the same attitude when it comes to being *spiritually* fit and prepared? If a guy like David can dedicate himself so fully to something that has value only for this life (and we're not trying to minimize the importance of what he does in any way), then why can't we dedicate ourselves to something that has value for this life *and* for eternity—and not just for us, but for all people everywhere?

Prepared for What?

A lot of Christians take the position that once they are saved, all they have to do is live their lives as quietly as possible so the big bad world doesn't contaminate them. They are like the misguided people who seal themselves and 14,000 cans of Bumble Bee tuna in a root cellar in Zortman, Montana, thinking the end of the world is at hand. The only good that does is to raise the revenues at Bumble Bee tuna. No one else benefits in the least. In his letter to the church at Ephesus, Paul came down hard on this kind of thinking.

> *So be careful how you live, not as fools but as those who are wise. Make the most of every opportunity for doing good in these evil days* (Ephesians 5:15,16).

"WHAT IF THE END OF THE WORLD IS AT HAND?"

When it comes to the Second Coming of Christ and the end of the world, don't get caught up in date setting, because Jesus said that no one but God knows the day or the hour when these things will happen (Matthew 24:36). But we can tell you this: *For each person on earth, the end of the world will occur in his or her lifetime.* We can say that with 100 percent certainty because the Bible says that each person must die once, and after that there's judgment (Hebrews 9:27). So when it comes to sharing your faith, you need to see each and every person as facing the end of the world when Jesus returns, or when they die, whichever comes first.

Stealth Christians

Other Christians take the position that once they are saved, there's nothing else to do. They try to blend quietly into society so that no one will notice the rather radical ideas Christians are sometimes known for. These stealth Christians think nothing of taking on some of the "harmless" habits and ways of the world. After all, God is a forgiving God, right? We've been saved by *grace*, not by works, so what's the big deal? There's freedom in Christ.

Oh boy, now you're messing where you shouldn't be messing. Paul was pretty direct when he wrote: "Don't be misled. Remember that you can't ignore God and get away with it. You will always reap what you sow!" (Galatians 6:7). Jesus was even more direct in His evaluation of stealth

Christians. To Jesus, a hypocrite (that's someone who professes one thing but practices another) was like a snake (Matthew 12:34).

On a more positive note, Jesus compared His followers to salt and light (Matthew 5:13-16). Just like you don't need a lot of salt to flavor a stew, the Christlike actions of a few people can influence great numbers. But what good is salt if it loses its flavor? Similarly, it only takes a single candle to light an entire room, but what good is your light if you keep it under wraps? Jesus wants us to let our light—which is the Good News and our good deeds—shine for all to see, "so that everyone will praise your heavenly Father (verse 16)."

Good-Smelling Christians

As Christians, we are called to be out in the open, living our lives for Jesus in whatever job or profession God has called us to do. Wherever we go, God wants to use us "to tell others about the Lord and to spread the Good News like a sweet perfume" (2 Corinthians 2:14). Yes, we need to take care of our families and be wise in how we live in difficult times, but our highest calling is to be salt, a light, and a good-smelling fragrance that attracts people to God.

As we live lives that are pleasing to God and attractive to people who are searching for meaning, we need to be ready to answer the questions they will certainly ask us about our lives, our faith, and our God.

So don't be afraid and don't worry. Instead, you must worship Christ as Lord of your life. And if you are asked about your Christian hope, always be ready to explain it (1 Peter 3:14,15).

Be Among the 5 Percent

Greg Laurie says that "95 percent of all Christians have never led another person to Christ." That's a sad and sobering statistic, because it probably means that 95 percent of all Christians aren't actively sharing their faith. What it also means is that 95 percent of all Christians are disobeying a direct order from Jesus, our Commander in Chief, who definitely told us to tell others about Him (see chapter 1).

Do you want to be in the 95 percent, or do you want to be among the 5 percent who share their faith and lead people to Christ? What we need to do is draw a line in the sand for ourselves and make a decision. Do we want to be like the guy in the root cellar, fat and afraid, hoping nobody knocks on the door? Or do we want to be like David the Navy Seal, fit and fearless, ready for anything and anyone that comes along?

"CHOOSE TODAY WHOM YOU WILL SERVE"

The great Old Testament military leader, Joshua, faced his people with a critical choice—would they serve the idols they used to serve, or would they honor and serve the Lord? "If you are unwilling to serve the LORD," Joshua said, "then choose today whom you will serve." Then Joshua stood tall and made a dramatic statement that should be on the lips of every serious Christian: "As for me and my family, we will serve the LORD" (Joshua 24:15).

One More Thing Before We Start

The first place to start as you prepare to share your faith is to pray for the lost. This is critical! If you want to have the heart of Jesus, you need to pray for the people Jesus died for.

> *I urge you, first of all, to pray for all people. As you make your requests, plead for God's mercy upon them, and give thanks....This is good and pleases God our Savior, for he wants everyone to be saved and to understand the truth* (1 Timothy 2:1,3,4).

Developing the Skills

Getting into spiritual shape is a lot like getting into physical shape. It takes time, effort, consistency, and discipline. Here's how the apostle Paul, one of history's most skilled Christians, explained it:

> *I don't mean to say that I have already achieved these things or that I have already reached perfection! But I keep working toward that day when I will finally be all that Christ Jesus saved me for and wants*

me to be. No, dear friends, I am still not
all I should be, but I am focusing all my
energies on this one thing: Forgetting the
past and looking forward to what lies
ahead, I strain to reach the end of the race
and receive the prize for which God,
through Christ Jesus, is calling us up to
heaven (Philippians 3:12-14).

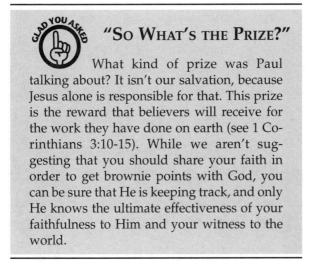

"So What's the Prize?"

What kind of prize was Paul
talking about? It isn't our salvation, because
Jesus alone is responsible for that. This prize
is the reward that believers will receive for
the work they have done on earth (see 1 Corinthians 3:10-15). While we aren't sug-
gesting that you should share your faith in
order to get brownie points with God, you
can be sure that He is keeping track, and only
He knows the ultimate effectiveness of your
faithfulness to Him and your witness to the
world.

Paul was one of the smartest people who
ever lived, and he was probably the
greatest missionary the world has ever

seen. Yet Paul never took the position that he had arrived. He was always learning more about God. Spiritually speaking, Paul was like a world-class athlete, yet he was always in training. We should approach our growth as Christians in the same way. Being "ready to explain" our faith is a work in progress, mainly because there's so much to learn.

Here's why: the more we know God—

✔ By discovering what He has done for us in the past

✔ By learning what He is doing in our lives now

✔ By understanding what He has planned for us in the future

—the more we realize how great He is and how much more we have to learn.

No eye has seen, no ear has heard, and no mind has imagined what God has prepared for those who love him (1 Corinthians 2:9).

Basic Training Part I—The Word of God

Just as there's no quick way to become a full-fledged Navy Seal, there's no quick way to become a fully equipped Christian. Oh, people try spiritual shortcuts all the time, but they never work:

✔ They watch television evangelists on a regular basis, hoping to get healthy, wealthy, and wise. What a shortcut Christian doesn't realize is that watching some guy in a white suit who flails his arms around won't help him or her grow as a Christian any more than watching a WWF wrestling match on TV will turn him or her into the next Stone Cold Austin.

✔ Shortcut Christians may go to church every week, but they never join a Bible study class or talk to the pastor. What they fail to understand is that simply "going" to church won't turn them into a super Christian any more than taking a Chevy Nova to a car wash will turn it into a Ferrari.

✔ Hoping to get that "Spirit-filled feeling," people looking for spiritual shortcuts find a tent meeting where people speak in tongues and flop around on the ground a lot. What they soon discover is that nobody knows what anyone else is saying. Besides, the average human skeletal structure can handle only so many "slayings."

✔ Shortcut Christians eventually stop going to church (because it's filled with hypocrites), and they rarely crack a Bible (because it's filled with "contradictions"). Instead, they read all of the "spiritual" titles on Oprah's book list, hoping to find meaning from within their own "spirit."

God's Training Manual

Don't get us wrong. There are many fine media programs with Christian themes that will help you grow. There are many wonderful churches in your community. You need to find one where you can worship God, fellowship with other Christians, and study the Bible. And there are Christ-centered books that will help equip you as a growing believer. But there's no substitute for getting your spiritual training directly from God.

We're not talking about voices in your head or visions in the night. God is available to train you through His personal training manual, the Bible. More than an ordinary book, the Bible contains the very words of God. The Bible is God's living message for you. It contains everything you need to live and grow as a Christian.

All Scripture is inspired by God and is useful to teach us what is true and to make us realize what is wrong in our lives. It straightens us out and teaches us to do what is right. It is God's way of preparing us in every way, fully equipped for every good thing God wants us to do (2 Timothy 3:16,17).

As you read the Bible daily, here are three things you should do:

✔ *Study* – Make an effort to systematically learn God's Word (2 Timothy 2:15).

✔ *Meditate* – Think deeply about God's Word (Psalm 1:2).

✔ *Memorize* – Be ready to recall God's Word (Psalm 119:11).

Not only will you please God when you read His message to you, but you will learn to:

✔ Live and grow as a Christian (1 Peter 2:2).

✔ Develop spiritual discernment (Acts 17:11).

✔ Answer the questions of others (1 Peter 3:15).

Basic Training Part II – The Spirit of God

Trying to share your faith without the Bible is futile. Sharing your faith without the Holy Spirit is foolish. This is because the Holy Spirit gives you power in at least three different ways. Without this power, the life you live and the words you say will fall totally flat.

1. The Holy Spirit Guides You

As a Christian, you have a tremendous advantage over the person who doesn't know God personally. You have the Holy Spirit in your life (1 Corinthians 12:13), and one of His primary functions is to "guide you into all truth" (John 16:13). This isn't your average, everyday truth (such as the truth that dogs have wet noses). This is truth about God and His ways. There is no greater truth!

But we know these things because God has revealed them to us by his Spirit, and his Spirit searches out everything and shows us even God's deep secrets (1 Corinthians 2:10).

2. The Holy Spirit Enlightens Others

The reason it's foolish to share your faith without the Holy Spirit is that the message of the gospel is foolish to anyone who doesn't know God personally (1 Corinthians 2:14). Do you ever wonder why nonbelievers often shake their heads when they hear Christians talk about God?

It's because their minds are literally blinded to the things of God. Unless the Holy Spirit opens their hearts and their minds to receive our message, nothing will happen. Here's what the apostle Paul wrote about preaching to the church at Corinth:

> *I came to you in weakness—timid and trembling. And my message and my preaching were very plain. I did not use wise and persuasive speeches, but the Holy Spirit was powerful among you. I did this so that you might trust the power of God rather than human wisdom* (1 Corinthians 2:3-5).

It's the power of the Holy Spirit—and not merely your words—that will ultimately lead someone to receive the message of the gospel. Remember, your job is to *proclaim* the Good News. It's up to the Holy Spirit to *convict* and *convince*.

> When you're witnessing to someone, you have to allow the Spirit of God to do His work. When you do that, you'll be encouraged and rewarded to know that the Holy Spirit will use you in the lives of those who don't know Christ.
> —John MacArthur

3. The Holy Spirit Prays When You Don't Know What to Pray For

Another incredible benefit of the Holy Spirit in your life is stated by Paul in his letter to the church in Rome:

> *And the Holy Spirit helps us in our distress. For we don't even know what we should pray for, nor how we should pray. But the Holy Spirit prays for us with groanings that cannot be expressed in words. And the Father who knows all hearts knows what the Spirit is saying, for the Spirit pleads for us believers in harmony with God's own will* (Romans 8:26,27).

Think about that for a minute. When you don't know how to pray or what to pray for, the Holy Spirit prays on your behalf in ways you can't even imagine. Is your heart burdened for an unsaved friend, yet you don't know what to say or how to pray? The Holy Spirit is way ahead of you. He is already praying to the Father for you and your friend.

Know What You Believe

When you first accept Jesus as your Savior, you have faith in a God you don't know very well. But as you "learn to know God better and better" (Colossians 1:10), your faith grows because you know more about your faith. This gives you greater confidence as you share your faith with others.

Along with reading the Bible, you should be reading books that help you better understand your faith. Start building your library with these books (we've listed some great titles at the end of this chapter). Meanwhile, here is our list of the Top Ten Fundamentals of the Christian Faith:

1. The Bible

The Bible is God's inspired, inerrant message to us. The Bible gives us direction (Psalm 119:105), shows us right and wrong (Psalm 119:11), and shows us the truth about ourselves (Hebrews 4:12).

2. God

God is the self-existent, infinite, holy, personal Creator of the universe. God has always existed, and He created the universe by the power of His Word (Hebrews 11:3). There is only one true God (Isaiah 45:5). In the unity of the Godhead there are three persons of one substance— the Father, the Son, and the Holy Spirit— with distinct personalities.

3. Jesus Christ

Jesus is the only begotten Son of God, yet completely God and one with the Father (John 10:30). Jesus is the Mediator between God and humankind, having been sent by God to earth to die for us and forgive our sins (John 1:29).

4. The Death and Resurrection of Jesus

Jesus died on the cross, was buried, and after three days rose from the dead (1 Corinthians 15:3,4). After forty days Jesus ascended into heaven, where He is at the right hand of the Father (Hebrews 1:3), pleading to God on our behalf (1 John 2:1).

5. Man and Sin

God created humans in His image (Genesis 1:26,27) with an eternal soul (Matthew 10:28). Our chief end is to glorify God and enjoy Him forever. Yet the entire human race falls short of God's perfect standard because of sin (Romans 3:23). Our sin leads to death, but God has given us eternal life through Jesus Christ (Romans 6:23).

6. Salvation

We are saved from our sins and death by believing in the person and work of Jesus Christ (John 3:16). There's nothing we can do to earn our salvation; it is God's gracious gift to us (Ephesians 2:8,9). Once you believe by faith that God has saved you by His grace in Jesus, you are secure in Christ for eternity (John 10:28,29).

7. The Holy Spirit

The Holy Spirit is the third person of the Godhead, who has always existed with God the Father and Jesus Christ. The Holy Spirit baptizes every believer into the body of Christ (1 Corinthians 12:13) and gives each of us spiritual gifts and empowers us to bear spiritual fruit when we give Him control of our lives (Galatians 5:22,23). The Holy Spirit is our guarantee that Jesus Christ is coming back for His church (2 Corinthians 1:21,22).

8. Angels, Satan, and Demons

There is a very real spirit world, made up of God's messengers, called angels, and God's enemies, Satan and his demons (Ephesians 6:12). Satan is also the enemy of the believer (1 Peter 5:8), and he blinds the mind of the unbeliever (2 Corinthians 4:4). Satan and his allies are ultimately doomed to defeat (Revelation 20:10).

9. The Church

The church is the universal body of Christ, comprised of all believers everywhere. The church exists so that we can worship God (Ephesians 5:16-19), serve one another (Ephesians 4:12), and share our faith (Mark 16:15).

10. Future Things

God has a plan for the future, which includes the end of the world as we know it and the creation of a new heaven and a new earth. The focal point of God's future plan is the Second Coming of Christ, which will happen unexpectedly (Matthew 24:44). Judgment and eternal life in hell await the unbeliever (Revelation 20:15). All those who have believed in Jesus Christ will spend eternity in heaven, which Jesus is preparing for us (John 14:1-3).

How to Share the Gift of Salvation

When you begin to actively share your faith with others, you will have many opportunities to explain God's plan of salvation. This is the highest privilege you can have as a believer. You will know when someone is ready to take the steps to knowing God personally. Here are six steps to knowing God that you can share when the time is right:

Step 1—God loves you and wants to have a relationship with you (John 3:16).

Step 2—You will never satisfy God's perfect standards (Romans 3:23).

Step 3—Jesus did something you could never do: He died for your sins (Romans 5:8).

Step 4—The only way to God is through Jesus (John 14:6).

Step 5—Jesus is knocking at the door of your heart (Revelation 3:20).

Step 6—You need to personally receive Jesus Christ into your life (Romans 10:9).

You may want to write these steps on a blank page in your Bible. Better yet, memorize the steps and the Bible verses so you can respond any time to someone who wants to connect with God personally.

What's That Again?

1. Dedicate yourself to becoming a spiritually fit Christian.

2. God is always available to train you through His personal training manual, the Bible.

3. The Holy Spirit is an essential part of your growth and witness as a Christian.

4. Know the basics of the Christian faith, and study them throughout your life.

5. The highest priority you can have as a believer is to share the steps to knowing God.

Dig Deeper

Here are three essential books to help you better understand your faith.

Know What You Believe by Paul Little. This classic book explains the fundamentals of the Christian Faith.

Nothing But the Truth by John MacArthur. What should you say when asked about your faith? This book provides solid, biblical answers.

Bruce & Stan's Guide to God by Bruce & Stan. This book gives you the basics of your faith in typical Bruce & Stan style.

Moving On

The first half of our book has covered the "nuts and bolts" of your faith and how you share it. Now it's time to look at the basics of your life and how you live it, because what you do speaks louder than what you say.

Chapter 3

Words Are Not Enough: What You Do Speaks Louder Than What You Say

Preach the Gospel at all times. When necessary, use words.

—St. Francis of Assisi

When people think about witnessing, they usually worry about the words they are going to say. The words you speak about Jesus are important. Words are used to *explain* how a person can establish a personal relationship with Jesus. Words can also be used to *describe* how Jesus transformed your life from the inside out. But words aren't the only method you have for witnessing, and often they aren't the most effective.

Don't think about witnessing only in terms of what you say. That perspective will make your concept of witnessing too narrow. Sure, witnessing includes talking to people about God. But it is more than that. Even if you aren't talking, you will be sharing your faith by the way you act and the things that you do. Yep, your conduct is one of the ways that you share your faith in God. In fact, your behavior—your lifestyle—is the most effective way for you to show people how God has changed your life. All of your words about the love of God will be useless if your lifestyle reflects a personality that is the opposite of love. But when you respond with love in a way that is completely opposite of human nature, then people will notice that your life is different. They'll want you to tell them what makes your life different. They will be anxious to hear your answer, and they'll listen to what you have to say. That is when the words become important, but it is only after you have witnessed to them through your actions.

In this chapter, we'll talk about the importance of making sure that your *walk* is consistent with your *talk*.

Bruce & Stan

Chapter 3

Words Are Not Enough: What You Do Speaks Louder Than What You Say

What's Ahead

➤ Close Encounters of the Chance and Continuing Kinds
➤ You Are a Witness 24 x 7
➤ Act Like Christ Before You Talk About Christ
➤ Loving Works Better Than Lecturing

*I*n the first two chapters of this book, we have focused on "sharing your faith" in the context of what you should *say* to someone about God. And isn't that what you have been worrying about all along—what *words* to use and when to say them? Well, with two chapters of this book ingrained in your cranium, we have some good news (and bad news) for you:

The Good News: We have told you all you need to know for sharing with someone the basics of being a Christian. You can stop worrying. You've got all the necessary words. (Hey, you could even rip a few pages out of chapter 2 and give them to a person if you ever get laryngitis or if your lips go numb.)

The Bad News: The "words" aren't the hardest part of sharing your faith. In fact, they are the easiest part. It is much harder to *live* your faith than to *explain* it.

Sharing your faith usually involves direct contact with people. The only way you can avoid this is if you:

✔ Do all of your witnessing by bulk mail to third world countries;

✔ Buy a cable television studio and broadcast your sermons at 3 A.M.; or

✔ Stick to telephone evangelism—read Bible verses to those folks who keep bugging you to change your long-distance carrier.

Otherwise, you're going to have to actually meet the people you talk to.

Close Encounters of the Chance and Continuing Kinds

We don't mean to oversimplify things, but all of the people with whom you could share your faith fall into two groups:

Chance Encounters of the Random Kind

These are the people that you will only see once, and then probably never again. This group includes:

✔ The lady waiting next to you at the airport;

✔ The guy standing ahead of you in the "12 items or less" line at the supermarket; and

✔ The gas station attendant who gives you directions when you are lost.

Of course, you should be ready to share your faith with these people, but often the circumstances don't seem just right for doing so.

✔ The lady at the airport heard you lose your temper at the counter when your flight was delayed. She saw you make the ticket agent cry. She cowers whenever you move toward her, so you probably won't be able to get close enough to talk with her about the inner peace that comes from knowing Jesus.

✔ You yelled at the guy in the grocery line because you counted the items in his cart, and he had 13 of them. Of course, he qualified to stay in the line after he threw a package of frozen peas at you.

✔ You're too rushed to talk to the gas station attendant. You have to make up for all that time you spent driving around before you worked up the nerve to ask someone for directions.

We aren't saying that you shouldn't try to share your faith with strangers. You should. And, if your conduct in that brief contact with them doesn't immediately ruin your credibility, the words you speak might answer one of their spiritual questions. Your reference to a personal relationship with God in that casual conversation might be the encouragement they need to start seeking God.

Chance encounters happen everyday, in all sorts of circumstances. But we think that sharing your faith will happen more with the other group of people.

Continuing Encounters of the Personal Kind

These are the people who see you all of the time. You keep running into them because they are in your network of relationships. This group includes:

✔ *The members of your family.* It is difficult to avoid this group because you share a refrigerator and a bathroom with them.

✔ *Your relatives and in-laws.* You see them only a few times a year, but sometimes that is more than enough. Even if they only come at Thanksgiving, you remember them all year long (because they left that cranberry sauce stain on the dining room carpet).

✔ *The people you go to school with or know from work.* Some of them may be your friends—others may be your enemies —but you see them almost every day.

✔ *The people in your neighborhood.* You may know some better than others, but your residential proximity means that you see them on a fairly regular basis.

These are the people who you are most likely to share your faith with. Why? Because you have the most contact with them. Actually, your continuing relationships are one of those "good news/bad news" situations. Here we go again:

The Good News: You see your continuing relationships on a frequent basis. You will have lots of opportunities to share your faith with them.

The Bad News: They see you all of the time. They know what kind of a person you are. They might not think much of what you say about Christianity if they don't think much of you.

With people who know you, the words you speak are not the only way that you share your faith about God. Before you even get the words out of your mouth, these people have already had an opportunity to observe your lifestyle. Their opinion of you—based on what they have observed—will influence them more about God than any words that you can say.

WHAT DOES IT MEAN TO BE A "WITNESS"?

As we discussed in chapter 1, the terminology for sharing your faith includes words like "witnessing" and "being a witness." Everyone is familiar with the concept of a "witness" in a courtroom trial (not the sleazy kind on television with the celebrity wannabe judges—we mean the legitimate ones). Well, it just so happens that Bruce is a lawyer (not the sleazy kind either). Bruce was glad to give his expert opinion on the definition of a "witness" (actually, he was glad until we told him that he couldn't charge a fee for it):

✔ A witness is someone who has information or knowledge of something.

✔ A person can be a witness without testifying in court. If a person sees a bank robbery or a car accident, he is a witness even though he refuses to testify. Just having personal information about the issue makes the person a witness.

✔ The jury doesn't have to accept what a witness says as being true. It is the job of the jury to determine whether the witness was credible and believable.

✔ A witness can be "impeached" if he says other things or acted in ways that are contrary to his testimony. An impeached witness is not believable.

As Christians, we aren't likely to be put in the witness box of a courtroom to testify about God. But we are witnesses because we have personal knowledge about Him. Here are some important questions: Are we credible witnesses? Can other statements we have made impeach our oral testimony about God? Have we acted in a manner that is contrary to our testimony about Christianity?

You Are a Witness 24 x 7

"Witnessing" doesn't just happen when you are explaining John 3:16 to someone. It happens all of the time, every moment of your life. If you are a Christian, you are a witness 24 hours a day, 7 days a week. During those hours, people are watching your reactions (okay, except during the hours when you are sleeping). All of those people who are your continual relationships see you every day. If they know you are a Christian (and they have a pretty good idea because you're always driving to church on Sunday mornings), then they are likely to evaluate Christianity based on your conduct on Mondays through Saturdays.

Whether You Want to Be or Not

Notice that this witness thing happens whether you want it to or not. Oh sure, we all want our unsaved family and friends to be paying attention to us when we go to church or volunteer at the Rescue Mission. In other words, we don't mind them scrutinizing our behavior when we are acting spiritual. But we sure don't want them noticing what we do and say when:

✔ We yell a few "unpleasantries" at the referee who made a bad call at our kid's soccer game;

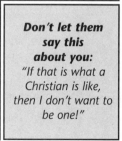

Don't let them say this about you: "If that is what a Christian is like, then I don't want to be one!"

✔ We're laughing at a crude and offensive joke; or

✔ A driver cuts us off on the freeway, and we mutter something about his intelligence, his upbringing, and his lineage.

These are just a few examples. We each have our own special set of sins that keep cropping up in our lives that we would be ashamed for people to see.

Are You a Credible Witness?

Go back and read the "What Does It Mean to Be a Witness?" box on page 67. Now imagine that you are talking about your faith in Jesus Christ with one of your unsaved friends. Is your testimony believable? Will your friend believe what you have to say based on how you have been living? Or will you be "impeached" as a witness because you are not practicing what you are preaching?

- **If you are living a consistent Christian lifestyle,** then you are a believable witness. Your friend will know that your faith is sincere because it has affected the way that you live.

- **If your lifestyle is inconsistent**—if your conduct doesn't reflect the principles of Christ—then your friend will think either:

> Christianity is a hoax. It doesn't work. Your life is proof of that.

> Or

> You don't really believe what you are talking about (because your life contradicts what you are saying). If *you* don't believe it, why should anyone else?

You can have the most eloquent and articulate oral presentation of the gospel, but it won't have much effect if the conduct of your life contradicts what you are saying.

ARE YOU LEAKING?

How do you know whether someone is good at an occupation? You look at the product of their work—what they have made. So:

- If you want to know whether Nick is a good farmer, you inspect his fields. Are the crops growing? Are there a lot of weeds? Are the irrigation rows leaking?

- If you want to know if John is a good plumbing contractor, you inspect one of the houses that he is building. Do the toilets flush? Are the pipes leaking?

- If you want to know whether Shannon is a good surgeon, you inspect one of her patients. Is he still living? Is he leaking?

You are the product of Christianity—you are what God has made. If people want to know whether Christianity is valid, they are likely to look at you. Are you leaking?

Act Like Christ Before You Talk About Christ

Except for those rare instances when you'll share your faith with a stranger (the "chance encounter"), effective witnessing involves a combination of your character, your conduct, and your communication. All of these aspects of your life should be a reflection of Jesus Christ. That is what witnessing is all about—telling and showing other people what Jesus is like. You can *tell* them by what you *say*, but you *show* them with your own conduct.

As Christians, we should be engaged in the ongoing effort to become more like Christ in our thoughts, deeds, and words. That is what is involved with witnessing. So, we are doing everything necessary for witnessing when we do what it takes to be a fully devoted follower of Christ. That is a process that involves:

- Pursuing the character of Christ;

- Practicing the deeds of Christ;

- Presenting the simplicity of Christ.

Pursue the Character of Christ

In his usual blunt fashion, the apostle Paul laid it on the line when he said:

Your attitude should be the same that Christ Jesus had (Philippians 2:5).

If you want to have the attitude and character of Christ, you have to change your whole way of thinking. You can't trust your natural instincts because they are the opposite of God's spiritual instincts. You can have a Christlike attitude only after God has been able to transform your thinking:

Let God transform you into a new person by changing the way you think. Then you will know what God wants you to do (Romans 12:2).

Being like Christ sounds impossible. Actually, it is if we try to do it by ourselves. But God, through the Holy Spirit, gives us the ability to be like Christ:

> *And as the Spirit of the Lord works within us, we become more and more like him and reflect his glory even more* (2 Corinthians 3:18).

As we give God more control of our lives, then we start to exhibit His character in our lives. The traits of Christ, as listed in Galatians 5:22,23, will start to pop out in our life. In a world that is filled with anger, selfishness, and hostility, people will start to notice something different about us when we exhibit:

✔ Love

✔ Joy

✔ Peace

✔ Patience

✔ Kindness

✔ Goodness

✔ Faithfulness

✔ Gentleness

✔ Self-control

You will be a believable witness to your unsaved family and friends when you talk about the love of God if they have seen these traits in your life.

How to Prove You Are a Follower of Christ

Jesus said that there was a way that we could become credible witnesses for Him and prove to the world that we are His followers. Interestingly, it isn't by declaring our allegiance to Him by any oath. The proof comes not from words but from our love for each other:

"Your love for one another will prove to the world that you are my disciples" (John 13:35).

Practice the Deeds of Christ

Do you remember the WWJD phenomenon? Maybe you still have a WWJD bracelet left in your desk drawer (or maybe still on your wrist). "What Would Jesus Do?" was not a gimmick invented by some Christian retailing consultant. Jesus is the One who started it when He said:

> *"I have given you an example to follow. Do as I have done to you"* (John 13:15).

In other words, being a witness for Christ—showing people what He is like—involves doing the kinds of things that He did.

Those who say they live in God should live their lives as Christ did (1 John 2:6).

Don't worry about trying to copy everything Jesus did. You don't have to start with walking on water or turning water into wine. Your unsaved family and friends might be more impressed if you:

✔ Don't retaliate when someone is rude to you;

✔ Make (or at least buy) a dinner for your neighbors when they are sick;

✔ Treat homeless people with dignity;

✔ Take time out of your busy schedule to help a friend move; or

✔ Give your seat on the commuter train to someone else.

There is no better way to explain the love of Christ than to be an example of the love of Christ.

DON'T WORRY IF YOU AREN'T PERFECT

No one expects you to be perfect. Not even your in-laws. It will be enough if you are making an honest attempt to be Christlike in your character and conduct. After all, part of telling people about God is the admission that none of us is perfect. D. T. Niles said it this way: "Christianity is one beggar telling another beggar where to find food."

Present the Simplicity of Christ

If you have been modeling the character and conduct of Christ, you will have established the credibility to talk about your faith with your family and friends who don't know about Him. In fact, they might be anxious to know what makes you "so different" than other people. As you explain what Jesus has done in your life, remember to keep it simple: Just tell them about Jesus.

Jesus said that we are supposed to be His witnesses (Acts 1:8). That means we just tell people what we know about Him. Plain and simple.

- ✔ *We aren't supposed to be Jesus' public relations agent.* He doesn't need us to build up a bunch of hype about Him. Don't alter what you have to say based on what you think your friends want to hear. Just tell them about Jesus as you know Him.

- ✔ *We aren't His sales force.* We aren't paid on a commission based on how many people we get to sign a "salvation" contract. There should be no pressure tactics.

- ✔ *He doesn't need a marketing strategist.* Don't think that you need to trick people into learning about Jesus. Be up-front and straightforward with people. Jesus can take it from there.

People don't need a religion, but they do need Jesus. Don't get distracted from this simple message: Jesus loves them, He died on the cross to pay the penalty for their sins, and He wants to establish a personal relationship with them.

Loving Works Better Than Lecturing

Leave the sermons to the pastors. Your friends and family don't want to hear any preaching from you. They don't need to be lectured, scolded, or ridiculed. You are not properly representing Jesus if you are alienating these people when you present the gospel message to them. Sure, they are sinners,but so are you. Jesus hated your sin, but He loved you. And you should show that same love to all of the unsaved people that you know.

Sharing your faith effectively—through your character, your

> The quality of your life is the sermon that you are preaching to the people who don't know Jesus.

conduct, and your words—is simply the natural outgrowth of loving God:

• As you love God more, you will be more excited about the things He is doing in your life. Your excitement about God will make it easier for you to talk to other people about Him.

• As you love God more, your understanding of Him will grow. Your relationship with Him will become even more personal. It will be easier for you to explain about your relationship with God to those who don't know Him.

• As you love God more, you won't have to force yourself to share your faith. You will be doing it naturally—your deeds and words will be a testimony of God's love—because the Holy Spirit is producing God's character in your life.

• As you love God more, you will begin to feel His love for the unsaved. You will be looking for opportunities to share God's love to family, friends, and strangers who are spiritually lost.

> *People don't care what you know, until they know that you care.*

"What's That Again?"

1. You should be prepared to talk with strangers about God, but you'll have the most opportunities to share your faith with the people you interact with on a regular basis.

2. The people who know you will look for consistency between what you say and the way that you live. You will be impeached as a witness for God if your lifestyle conflicts with your testimony.

3. Sharing our faith involves a lot more than just the words that we speak. It also involves consistency in our character and conduct.

4. Effective witnessing requires that we:
   - Pursue the character of Christ;
   - Practice the deeds of Christ; and
   - Present the simplicity of Christ.

5. Sharing your faith will be a lot easier if you forget about lecturing people. Instead, try loving them. That will happen naturally as you love God more.

Dig Deeper

These books discuss the practical aspects of sharing your faith.

- *How to Give Away Your Faith* by Paul Little. This book is the "classic." You'll find it very helpful.

- *Lifestyle Evangelism* by Joe Aldrich describes how you can make evangelism a natural part of your lifestyle.

- *Out of the Salt Shaker & Into the World* by Rebecca Manley Pippert. This book explains how we can build relationships that will allow us to share our faith with credibility.

Moving On

We sense that you are still worried about something. You're thinking…"What if people ask me a tough question that I can't handle? What if they argue with me? What if they humiliate me?"

Those are great questions, but you don't need to freak out. In the next chapter we will talk about how you can handle objections and the people who reject you.

Chapter 4

WHEN THEY HUFF AND THEY PUFF:
HANDLING OBJECTIONS AND REJECTIONS

We cannot pander to a man's intellectual arrogance, but we must cater to his intellectual integrity.

—John Stott

This last chapter may be the most important one for you. We know that this whole witnessing thing has you worried. Maybe we don't know *exactly* what has your gastrointestinal tubes in a knot, but we have a pretty good idea. Come on. After all we have been through together, you can't hide anything from us. We feel your hands shaking. We see the blood vessels pulsating in your eyeballs.

Sharing your faith takes *words*, but that is the easy part. (You could just memorize John 3:16 and leave it at that.) But the hard part of witnessing is finding the nerve to open your mouth. Is that what's troubling ya, Bunky?

Perhaps you're worried that someone will reject you (and your message). Or, maybe you're fretting that someone will raise an objection that you can't answer. Well, if these issues are what have you worried, then join the club. We were the charter members.

But the fear of rejection and objections can be easily overcome when you understand a few basic principles about dealing with skeptics and their questions. So, put down that bottle of Pepto-Bismol, stop chewing on those antacid tablets, and cancel that prescription for ulcer medication. If we can share our faith without "losing our lunch," so can you.

Bruce & Stan

Chapter 4

When They Huff and They Puff: Handling Objections and Rejections

● ●

What's Ahead

➤ What Are You Afraid Of?
➤ The Great Things About Skeptics
➤ Questions and Objections You'll Love to Answer
➤ What Are You *Really* Afraid Of?
➤ A Few Things You Shouldn't Forget

● ●

*I*n your various conversations each day, you talk about a lot of different topics. Some of them are noble (such as your suggestions for solving the homeless problem) and some of them are mundane (such as discussing whether the McDonald's special for 39 cent hamburgers is on Wednesdays or Thursdays). But whether you are talking about politics, or sports, or movies, or the implications of a

flat tax, or whatever, you can be sure of
two things:

• The person you are talking to is not
  going to agree with you 100 percent on
  everything you are talking about. The
  two of you are bound to have a difference of opinion on a few issues.

• You don't have all of the available information about each subject you are
  talking about. You know a lot about a
  few topics, and a little bit about some
  others. But there is not a subject on
  which you have all of the answers.
  That's okay. Your limited knowledge
  doesn't make you afraid to participate
  in the discussion. In everyday conversations, we talk about a lot of different
  topics.

So why is it then, that we all choke on our
Altoids (you know, those curiously strong
peppermints) when the conversation turns
to God? Are we afraid that the person we
are talking to will disagree with what we
say? Are we afraid we'll be asked a question that we can't answer? If we don't have
these fears when we are talking about

other topics, why are we so uptight about talking about spiritual matters?

What Are You Afraid Of?

It seems that most of us Christians have an inordinate fear when it comes to sharing our faith. (That's right, you aren't alone in this. We're right in there with you.) So, let's ask ourselves the obvious question: What are we so afraid of?

We Are Way Too Psycho About Witnessing. As we try to analyze our fears, maybe it seems that we are being a little psychotic, and way too paranoid:

- **We have an irrational fear of humiliation.** What if someone makes fun of us for having a belief in God? They might say that religion is for weaklings. We just couldn't bear it if they called us . . . a "sissy." How could we ever walk out in public if everyone is whispering "There goes a sissy-pants" when we walk by? Oh, the shame of it all.

- **We have an irrational fear of rejection.** What if the people that we are talking to are so offended by what we say that they don't want to be our friends anymore? What if they run around telling everyone else we know that we are wild-eyed religious fanatics? And then what if everyone we know rejects us? We will be ostracized from society. We will be friendless. We'll have to sit by ourselves on the curb outside at Starbucks while our former so-called friends hang out inside. They will be the "cool" people and we will be the outcasts. After a while, Starbucks won't even serve us anymore. We'll have to get our coffee at . . . Denny's! And they don't have vanilla lattes at Denny's—they just have plain old coffee in those round Pyrex things. Oh, the indignity of it all.

- **We have an irrational fear of embarassing God.** After all that God has done for us, we want Him to be proud of us. We wouldn't want to do anything that embarrasses Him. So, we wouldn't want to talk about Him to the people we hang out with, because what if we are asked a question about God that we can't answer? If we can't answer a question, it will make us look dumb, and since we are a "child of God," then our friends might think that our spiritual stupidity is an inherited trait. That would mean that they'll think God is dumb, too. If we make God look dumb, He is going to be really ticked at us. He might even send a plague our way. (Hey, we read the Old Testament. We know He can be a God of wrath. We can do just fine without locusts or boils, thank you very much.)

What Is the Worst That Could Happen?
Let's look at this whole thing rationally for a moment. It just isn't realistic to think that sharing your faith will cause total calamity in your life. You won't end up living on the streets with no friends, locusts in your pants, and only your boils to keep you company. What is the worst that could happen?

- **Someone may disagree with you.** Big deal. So what? You don't have an emotional breakdown when you argue about politics or who is going to win the Super Bowl. Sure, we know that a person's salvation is really serious. We aren't intending to demean or trivialize Christ's death on the cross by comparing it to the Super Bowl. But we are talking about you and your hesitancy to talk about God because of an unwarranted fear of rejection and humiliation. All we're saying is that a difference of opinion is nothing new for your friends. It won't shock them, and it probably won't offend them. They will still think you're a nice person. You'll still get invited to Starbucks.

- **You might not have a great answer for every question.** Not having an answer or two is better than being viewed as a "know-it-all." People will actually respect you if you are willing to admit that there are a few things about God that you don't know or understand. (That's one of the things that makes God so amazing—we can't know everything about Him.) If someone stumps you with an honest question, make a promise to find out the answer. (Ask someone from your church for help.) Now you've got a reason to talk with that person again about God.

THERE ARE SOME QUESTIONS YOU DON'T NEED TO WORRY ABOUT

There is always some joker who will ask you a stupid question. Don't waste any time trying to figure out answers to questions like:

✔ Did Adam have a belly button?

✔ Where did Noah put the termites on the ark?

✔ Can God make a rock so heavy that He can't lift it?

These questions aren't legitimate obstacles to believing in God for this buffoon; he is just trying to rattle your cage.

The Great Things About Skeptics

At the risk of oversimplifying, we'll divide the unsaved people of the world into two categories:

• Seekers: These are people who are already "God-sensitive." They know there is a spiritual dimension to life, and they are looking for answers. Seekers are easy to talk to about God because they want to hear what you have to say. They are usually more anxious to listen than you are to talk.

• Skeptics: These are tough nuts to crack. They are so hard to convince. Many times they don't even want to get into a discussion about spiritual matters.

Now, you might think that hanging out with the seekers and avoiding the skeptics would be a more effective use of your time. It is natural to think that way because it would make your witnessing easier. But don't shun the skeptics. There are some really great reasons why you need to share your faith with them:

1. Just in case you forgot, skeptics are going to hell unless they connect with Jesus. Somebody needs to talk with them about Him.

2. Talking with skeptics can actually strengthen your faith. They may force you to deal with issues and questions about Jesus and Christianity that you ignored or glossed over in your own

personal spiritual journey. Don't be afraid to explore these issues. It won't shake your faith because you already know the truth. And you've got the Holy Spirit on your side to help you come to the correct conclusion on these tough issues:

> *"He [the Holy Spirit] will guide you into all truth"* (John 16:13).

3. Skeptics have strong feelings and opinions about Jesus. That's good, even though their attitude toward Christ is a negative one. Their intensity against spiritual matters makes them good candidates to receive the gospel. They will want to challenge what you say and believe about Christ. If they approach the challenge with intellectual integrity, they will have to look at the evidence about Christ and consider all that He said and did. God has promised that He will be found by those who are honestly looking for Him:

> *"If you look for me in earnest, you will find me when you seek me. I will be found by you," says the LORD* (Jeremiah 29:13,14).

4. As you interact with skeptics, you will gain confidence in your ability to share your faith. You'll begin to realize that the Holy Spirit guides your thoughts and your responses. You'll recognize that most of the objections fall into a few basic categories which can be easily answered (see the following section).

Use a little discretion in the midst of dealing with skeptics. If you just became a Christian, you probably shouldn't challenge your atheist college philosophy professor to a debate at the half-time show at a basketball game. Similarly, you might want to decline an invitation to appear as a guest on *Politically Incorrect* if you are a brand new Christian and the other guests are the Chairman of the American Communist Party and the top lawyer for the ACLU.

In your own network of friends, any skeptics aren't likely to be hostile toward you (or toward Christianity) if you have been living a life that reflects the love of Jesus. Oh, they still might argue with your viewpoints, but they'll respect the sincerity of your beliefs because you have the lifestyle that gives your faith credibility. And that is what witnessing is all about—having established a rapport with people and having earned their respect so that you have the opportunity to be heard.

SOME REALLY FAMOUS CHRISTIANS STARTED OUT AS SKEPTICS

Skeptics who become Christians usually have a very strong faith because they really tested the claims of Christianity before they made their decision.

✔ One of the very first skeptics was Saul, who later was known as the apostle Paul. He was persecuting and killing Christians before he had his encounter with Christ. You can't get much more skeptical than that.

✔ C. S. Lewis is a renowned theologian. His books, *The Screwtape Letters* and the *Chronicles of Narnia* series, are Christian classics. C. S. Lewis was a skeptic who tried to disprove the existence of God. Guess what happened?

✔ *Evidence That Demands a Verdict* is one of our favorite books for looking at the logical reasons to believe in Jesus. The author, Josh McDowell, knows a lot about the objections of skeptics, because he used to be one.

Questions and Objections You'll Love to Answer

As you spend time talking to skeptics about their "problems" with Christianity, we think you'll discover an interesting phenomenon: There are only a few basic objections and questions. Skeptics may articulate their disbelief in different ways, but most of the time these are all variations on the same basic issues. Here are seven of the most common ones:

Seven Sayings of a Skeptic (with our hints for how you might respond)

#1. The Skeptics Ask: Can you prove that God exists? The pat answer is "Well, you can't prove that He doesn't exist." That's true, but resist pat answers because skeptics aren't persuaded by them (and you don't want to reduce the discussion to a level of sarcasm). Remember that you are talking to a skeptic who has been raised in a society of "postmodernism" which believes that there is no God and no absolute truth. With that kind of a philosophical background, the question is an honest one.

Don't let this question shake you. Just look around. The cosmos at large, and the human body and mind in particular, are ample proof that there was an intelligent designer at work in the universe. If your skeptic is a fan of Darwin and says that all that exists is the result of a few random molecules colliding together by chance, then we suggest that you both read a book like *Darwin on Trial* by Phillip Johnson that examines the question of God's existence from a scientific approach. (Tell your skeptic friend that Phillip Johnson is a professor from U.C. Berkeley. It's true, and most skeptics love Berkeley professors.)

#2. *The Skeptics Ask: How can a loving God allow evil and suffering in the world?*
This does sound sort of incongruous, doesn't it? Look at the inconsistencies from the skeptic's point of view:

✔ Tragic things happen to innocent people. (Babies are born with deformities; children are dying of starvation;

and around the world people are suffering under the rule of oppressive
governments.)

✔ And just as contradictory, good things
happen to bad people. (In our own
country, murderers escape justice; and
on the international scene, tyrants like
Saddam Hussein live in luxury.)

✔ To someone who lacks a biblical perspective of the world, it would seem
that either God doesn't care, or He is
powerless to do anything about it.

You should compliment the skeptic for
asking such an insightful question.

Let's be honest that some things do seem
unfair. As Christians we know that God is
pure love, so we can trust His judgement
in these circumstances. But the skeptic
doesn't trust God (yet), so what is a rea-
sonable response?

The Bible says that evil exists in the world
because mankind has chosen to rebel
against God. There is a "sin" virus in every
human. That is where evil finds its source.
In some people, the evil is contained in

large part; in others, the evil is expressed without restrictions. If God were to eliminate all of the evil from the world, He would obliterate humanity off the face of the earth. But God has not ignored the condition of wickedness and anguish in the world. Through Jesus Christ, God has provided a way for us to have eternal life in heaven where there will be no evil or suffering. In the perspective of eternity, our life on earth is only momentary. Through a relationship with Christ, we can be assured of an eternal life in heaven. And while we are stuck here on earth, God gives us spiritual strength and perspective to deal with the tough times in life:

> *Don't worry about anything; instead, pray about everything. Tell God what you need, and thank him for all he has done. If you do this, you will experience God's peace, which is far more wonderful than the human mind can understand. His peace will guard your hearts and minds as you live in Christ Jesus* (Philippians 4:6,7).

#3. The Skeptics Ask: How can a loving God send people to hell? This question can be easily answered when you realize that its premise is incorrect. God does not send people to hell. Hell is what they deserve because of their sin. They are going to hell on their own. But, because God is loving, He has provided a way to rescue them.

HEY, SKEPTIC—DON'T MISS THE BOAT!

Stan likes to describe God's plan of salvation by making an analogy to the movie *Titanic*. After the mighty ship had submerged, Rose was clinging to a piece of wood in the freezing water. A lifeboat floated by in the darkness to rescue the passengers from their peril. Rose would have surely died if she hadn't blown the whistle to be rescued.

In the spiritual dimension of lives, we are drowning and will surely die from the effects of our sin. Jesus didn't throw us in the water. He isn't sending us to our death. Just the opposite. He is the lifeboat. If we call out to Him, He will save us.

#4. The Skeptics Ask: What about people who have never heard about Jesus? This is a question that doesn't occur only to skeptics. A lot of Christians wonder about this issue. Since Christ's death on the cross

2000 years ago, there must have been millions of people who have lived and died without hearing the gospel message. And even in our own generation of satellite television broadcasts, there must be remote villages in China that don't have the luxury of electricity or missionaries. So, what happens to all of those people who die without having a chance to make a decision about God?

If you are looking to Bruce and Stan for the definitive answer, you are going to be disappointed. We don't have just one, complete, authoritative answer. But we have several partial answers. First, we know that God is just and fair. We can have confidence in His attributes (His character traits) that some people are not being treated unfairly. Secondly, the Bible says that there is enough evidence in nature to make God's existence obvious to anyone. (Check out Romans 1:19,20 and Psalm 19.)

The fact that we can't provide a satisfactory answer for this question isn't a legitimate excuse for rejecting Christ. (The Bible says that some aspects of God are kept secret from mankind. See Deuteronomy

29:29.) At the end of the world, when the skeptics stand before Jesus at the time of judgement, there will be no "Get Out of Hell Free" cards issued to them. The only relevant question at that time will be how they responded to Jesus, not how God handled the Chinese in that remote village.

#5: *The Skeptics Ask: How can the Bible be trusted when it has so many inconsistencies?* You can have a lot of fun with this one, but go easy. Ask your skeptic friends for an example of the inconsistencies that are bothering them. Usually, people don't know of any inconsistencies; they have just heard that as a common criticism, so they are repeating it.

The reliability of the Bible has been challenged over the centuries. If there was any evidence that truly discredited the Bible, it would be highly publicized. Actually, the contrary is true. All recent archeological discoveries have proven that the Bible is accurate and reliable from a historical point of view.

If your skeptic has legitimate, sincere questions about the content of the Bible, they probably can be explained by an understanding of:

✔ **How the Bible was written.** The Holy Spirit inspired the various authors. So they wrote God's message, but in their own vernacular and from their own perspectives. For example, there are differences in the four New Testament biographies about Jesus (Matthew, Mark, Luke, and John). The differences have nothing to do with errors or inconsistencies. It's just that the authors had such differences in backgrounds. (You can't get much more diverse than a tax collector, a physician, and a fisherman.)

✔ **How the Bible was transcribed.** There is an interesting history about how God's Word has been preserved and passed from the ancient scrolls. Scholars of ancient literature acknowledge the accuracy in the transcription of the various manuscripts.

✔ **How the Bible has been translated.** Different translations don't make the Bible unreliable. As culture changes, so does the language. Contemporary translations rely on the ancient manuscripts and the most current linguistics.

#6. The Skeptics Object: Christianity is too intolerant. By this objection, the skeptics are usually referring to the fact that Christ claimed to be the only way to reach God. They are right about that:

I am the way, the truth, and the life. No one can come to the Father except through me (John 14:6).

And that undeniable truth is a major tenent of the Christian faith:

There is salvation in no one else! (Acts 4:12).

But Christianity excludes no one. It is available to everyone who believes. It is totally inclusive:

For God so loved the world (John 3:16).

He [God] does not want anyone to perish (2 Peter 3:9).

Yes, God is intolerant of sin, but He excludes no sinner from His free gift of salvation.

#7. *The Skeptics Object: Christians are a bunch of hypocrites.* This is a legitimate criticism by skeptics. By and large, we Christians are a bunch of hypocrites. We talk about love and forgiveness, but we are often caught being spiteful and judgmental. But that is a criticism about us; it isn't a valid excuse for rejecting Christ. The fact that God loves us despite our imperfections (and our continual failings) illustrates God's grace.

HEY, SKEPTIC—DON'T DROP THE BALL!

If visitors from a foreign country wanted to understand the game of American football, you would take them to see a college game or to see two NFL teams play each other. You wouldn't take them to see a flag football game at the local elementary school. Why? Because those little third graders don't give a fair representation of how the game is supposed to be played. They aren't very skilled yet, and they are easily distracted (often more interested in the snack shop than the game itself).

> Skeptics who are really interested in knowing about Christianity should be examining the person of Jesus Christ. The rest of us are just learning how to play the game; hopefully, we keep improving, but Christ is the role model that the skeptics should be looking at.

What Are You Really Afraid Of?

Many Christians are hesitant to share their faith, but the fear of tough questions and objections is not the *real* reason. Most of us are just embarrassed that at times our Christian faith doesn't seem to be working. We don't feel any of the "joy" that is supposed to come from knowing Jesus. We don't want to admit this fact to non-Christians—it remains our own little secret. We appreciate that Christ died for us, so we don't want to talk about the tough times in Christianity because we wouldn't want Him to look bad. So, we just fake it! And we are afraid to share about our faith if we are just a bunch of big fakes.

 Well, if you feel like this, we want to take the pressure off of you. Jesus never promised that your Christian life would be easy. In fact, He said that we would be carrying a cross on a daily basis (Luke 9:23). But you need to be talking to God and to other Christians when life is getting tough for you. Christianity is not an individual sport; it is played as a team. The New Testament refers to Christians as being members of a family or as being different parts of the same body. If your Christian life isn't working like you think it should, chances are that the problem is with you. You need to be praying with God and talking with other Christians so you can get back on track.

We think you will have a completely different perspective about Christianity when you learn to talk with God and other Christians about the things that are weighing you down. You'll realize a completely different, dynamic aspect of the Christian life. You'll know God is with you to comfort and guide you, and He'll be using other Christians to encourage you. When this happens in your life, you'll be truly excited about God. You won't have to fake it anymore. Your faith and trust in God will be genuine—and you'll be glad to tell others about it.

A Few Things You Shouldn't Forget

Well, before we leave you, there are a few things we want you to remember:

- You aren't responsible for persuading or convincing people to accept Christ. You are just responsible for telling them about Him.

- This whole witnessing thing isn't even about you. And it isn't even about the person you are talking to. It is about Jesus. He is supposed to be the center of your attention.

- People can learn a lot about what you really believe by the way you live your life.

- You'll get better at sharing your faith the more often that you do it.

There are a few people who are dying to hear about Christ. The others may not be interested in hearing about Him, but they'll be dying if they don't.

Bruce & Stan

"What's That Again?"

1. Most of our fears about witnessing are irrational. You probably aren't going to be ridiculed or ostracized (maybe, but not likely).

2. About the worst thing that will happen is that somebody will disagree with you or ask a question. And the best thing that could happen would be for you to introduce them to Jesus. You should risk the worst thing for the chance to get the best thing.

3. Don't avoid the skeptics. Most of them ask honest questions. If they are asking with intellectual integrity, your responses can lead them to Christ.

4. Most of the questions asked by skeptics fall into a few basic categories. If you familiarize yourself with these few issues, then you don't have to worry about being caught off guard.

5. If you can't answer a tough question, don't sweat it. There are people in your church and lots of other resources available to help you learn the appropriate response. And by the way, you aren't expected to know everything. All you need to do is share your own personal experience with Christ.

Dig Deeper

Here are resources for dealing with the questions of skeptics. We have some great recommendations for you:

- *The Case for Christ* by Lee Strobel. With a background as a lawyer and journalist, Strobel was skeptical as he examined the evidence about Jesus. At the end of his investigation, he was convinced that Jesus was the Son of God. (Big surprise.)

- *Talking Truth Next Door* by David Faust reviews answers to questions that seekers are likely to ask.

- *Finding Common Ground* by Tim Downs. This book includes practical discussions for finding ways to discuss spiritual matters in the context of everyday life.

Moving On

Sharing your faith is primarily a matter of *living* your faith. And as you are in conversation with other people, witnessing is nothing more than simply talking naturally about the spiritual dimension of life.

If you can share your excitement about watching a basketball game, or seeing a good movie, or eating at a great restaurant, we know that you can talk about how God has been helping you through tough times. When you talk about God as a natural and important part of your life, then people will begin to ask you questions. Just tell them what you know from your own personal experience. That's better than any sermon they could hear at a Sunday worship service (because it is your personal story, and besides, they probably aren't going to church on Sundays anyway).

Don't forget to let us know how things are going for you. We're excited to hear about your experiences because we know exactly what will happen. As you begin to share your faith, you'll get more excited about your relationship with God. As your love for God grows more intense, you'll want to talk about Him even more. When you get that cycle going in your life, finding the words to say and the courage to speak will not be a problem for you anymore.

So, stop reading and start sharing.

About the Authors

Bruce Bickel is a lawyer, but he didn't start out that bad. After college, he considered the noble profession of a stand-up comic, but he had to abandon that dream because he is not very funny. As a lawyer, he makes people laugh (but it is not on purpose).

Stan Jantz is a retail-marketing consultant. From the time he was a little kid, Stan's family owned a chain of Christian bookstores, so he feels very comfortable behind the counter.

Bruce and Stan spend their free time as "cultural observers" (they made that term up). They watch how God applies to real life. Together they have written 20 books, and they host a weekly radio program, *The Bruce & Stan Show.* (Gee, you've got to wonder how they came up with that catchy title.)

Bruce and Stan would enjoy hearing from you. (If you've got something nice to say, then don't hold back. If you have a criticism, then be gentle.) The best way to contact them is:

E-mail: *guide@bruceandstan.com*
Snail Mail: Bruce & Stan
P.O. Box 25565
Fresno, CA 93729-5565

You can learn more than you ever wanted to know about Bruce and Stan by visiting their Web site:
www.bruceandstan.com